LAYING
IT ON
THICK

And Other Poems on Belief,
Belonging and Biblical Hope

RUPERT GREVILLE

With illustrations by Jennie Bradshaw

Illustrations by Jennie Bradshaw
Front cover and page design by Liz Carter

Contents

Abstract Themes 81

Miscellaneous Poems 111

ACKNOWLEDGEMENTS

In the practicalities of putting together this collection of poems, I'd like to thank Liz Carter whose skills have been deployed in the formatting of my manuscript, and making the book presentable in its current form. Many thanks to Jennie Bradshaw for her thoughtful work in illustrating my poems. I am also grateful to Rev. Nigel and Frances Richardson for their keen interest in my poems and their wise advice in assembling and presenting them as a book.

There are many others who have played their part in my writing journey, whether by patient listening to my readings, helpful comment on content and style, or general encouragement to press on with it. In particular, I'd like to mention Bobbie Cole, John Wakeman and our East Kent Association of Christian Writers (ACW) group, where generosity of spirit combines with challenge and practical writing advice. Also, the late Colin Pavey who, with his wife Olive, used to lead our Wednesday afternoon meeting at One Church, Dover. It was here that a number of these poems had their first readings.

Readers might detect themes and ideas in my poems influenced by the author NT Wright, whose work I am heavily indebted to and deeply grateful for. But there are many others who have played their part in my journey over the years. Charles Farrar-Bell was the Maths teacher who first encouraged me as a teenager to engage seriously with the Bible; Nick and Grace Turner the ones whose faith, teaching and example in family life encouraged me towards a fuller grasp of God's compassion for the world.

Aside from the many friends, writers and pastors who have encouraged me in faith and church life along the way, I'd like to thank my wife, Caroline, for all that she's given me of constructive feedback and interest in this project, but also to acknowledge her own love of Jesus and the compassionate heart that springs from her deep grasp of biblical truth. I can scarcely find words, let alone a rhyme, to express what a blessing she and our children are to me.

GENERAL INTRODUCTION

"What do you think of God?" I wasn't prepared for this blunt interrogation as I sat down to eat one evening with an elderly couple, and I felt a little ambushed. I was eighteen, and they weren't to know that I had spent my teenage years curious about the Christian faith. I had read my Gideons New Testament, and I had prayed too, at times. I had attended Christian holiday camps and been a regular attendee of my school Bible study meetings, but here I was on the cusp of adulthood, sitting solidly on the fence, suspicious of the Church, still wary of being "sucked in" by any kind of religious group. I remember mumbling to them something about my general belief in God, but that I didn't think there was enough actual proof around the Christian claims for me to commit my own life to them.

It wasn't many months after that conversation that I had a personal experience of what I believe to be the voice of Jesus as I lay awake late one night. It was a wonderfully clear and perfect pronunciation of my name that I heard: "Rupert", not judging, angry, cold or distant, but loving, kind and gentle. Having looked around the room to see who was there, I answered (a little embarrassed), asking what he wanted to say to me. I heard nothing more. I reflected on what had just happened. It *had* just happened, and I couldn't deny it. I knew this to be a biblical experience, and that everything conveyed in the way my name was spoken lined up with the character of Jesus, as related in the gospels. I thought about the purity of the sound that I had heard. It was completely undistorted, as I imagine sound would be through the highest quality headphones. I also reflected on his pronunciation of the two syllables of my name. I had never heard it spoken so beautifully.

I had not asked for such a direct and personal encounter. But this, I think, was the point. I would have liked objective and empirically verifiable evidence, that just said "there is a God", or "Jesus rose from the dead". What I received was something deeply relational, telling me (as I had already understood from the New Testament, but been unwilling to internalise) that he was indeed God, but that he was near and that he knew me, loved me, and forgave me.

As with the Church's testimony of Jesus down through the ages, mine is simply that I know him to be true. I cannot prove the veracity of my experience to anyone else, as no one else was there to share in it. I only know that for me to have denied it, dismissed it, or attributed it to anything other than the risen Jesus of the Bible, either at that time or at any time since, would have been utterly dishonest.

This is the only occasion that I have ever experienced his voice in this way. I have since met believers who have told me similar stories about their own encounters with Jesus, and I've read of others. I'm simply grateful that he reached out to me in the way that he did, and at that time, with such love and compassion. In these pages I hope that my poems and reflections convey that love.

You might be wondering why I became curious about God as a teenager in the first place. It was mostly because it seemed to me that nobody wanted to talk about him (except vicars, but they were paid to do it). I sang hymns and Christmas carols willingly enough, but I had little grasp of why their writers had been so "religious" that they'd felt the need to compose them.

I was fascinated that there actually were real, modern people who had real faith in the God of the Bible. Some of them even wrote books about him! It was through the kindness that I experienced among believing Christians, along with my own Bible reading (and some of those books), that I was able to explore for myself and, eventually, take hold of their message.

All that was over thirty years ago, but more recently I have felt especially motivated to compose rhymes of my own on biblical themes. I had been writing rhymes for a long time, usually for my children, and they'd generally been silly. I have tried to avoid silliness here, but there is an element of playfulness in some of them.

If the same curiosity that I had as a boy is there for you, maybe there's something in this collection that will help you to unpack aspects of Christian belief, and the meaning for us today of Jesus's coming two thousand years ago. *Belief* (in the risen Jesus and his victory over evil), *belonging* (to the worldwide community of believers) and *biblical hope* are all essential elements for Christian life. As with fire, with its dependence on fuel, heat and oxygen, if any one of the three elements are removed, it will falter. It may fizzle out altogether.

Not all Christian poetry has to centre on Bible verses, tell Bible stories or argue for Christian points of view. But this, mostly, has been my own journey in writing, arising from a strong desire to encourage and affirm Christian faith in others. Christian things are laid on thick in this book, and this will not be to everybody's taste.

But for those who do read my poems, whether you're just dipping in or outright bingeing, I hope that they will provoke thought around their various topics, lead you deeper into their relevant Bible themes, and that you will enjoy their presentation. Most of all, I hope that they will be read with hearts open simply to the Good News that the Messiah came, died, and was raised from the dead. His life today, and his love for us, and his interest in us as we each live out our own lives, demands a response from us. I would be thrilled if this collection of poems were to help fuel in your heart a desire, perhaps for the first time, to know him and to worship him.

Some of the poems imagine characters and situations described in the Old and New Testaments, some cover broader biblical themes, while others seek to challenge frequently encountered worldviews from a Christian perspective, or at least, from mine. In all of them, and in my comments and choices of scripture that accompany them, I hope that I fall into the "2 Timothy, 2:15" category of writers: neither ashamed of the Christian message, nor guilty of mishandling the "word of truth".

To the non-believer, I would wish you to read these words as my testimony to who Jesus is, who I know him to be, and not as mere regurgitation in rhyme of Christian sentiment. To the Christian believer, may they be an encouragement for you to pursue deeper, richer relationship with Jesus. He is able to meet us - whether we're the hardened centurion, or the broken, desperate lady who secretly touches his cloak for healing – to restore us and to offer us new purpose and hope.

What do you think of God? It's a question for all of us, the buttered-side-up kind of people as much as the buttered-side down – and everyone in between. For my part, much like the man who invented alphabet butter, I'm just excited to be spreading the word.

Faith and Scepticism

LAYING IT ON THICK

Tell us, What's the Christian stance?
We'd like to hear your case:
Isn't life just random chance
and meaningless in space?
You have our whole attention
drawn completely to your views -
Enlighten us and brighten us
in any way you choose.

Well, to st….

Talk about the Bible,
and explain what it's about,
With everyone so tribal
and the Hebrews winning out;
Take us through the Torah
and the prophets and the kings,
The Jewish diaspora,
and the sacrificial things.

OK, so the Bib….

Hold forth about your Saviour;
lay it on us super-thick;
Confront our bad behaviour
with your saving gospel schtick;

Defend your own belief in him;
say why he's not a fraud -
Why reasons for receiving him
are multi-layered and broad.

Right, well Je....

Except, don't. Just don't.
Just talk about the weather.
If you can't do that, or won't, of course,
we'll not get on together.
I know you'd like to share it,
that you'd love to hold the floor,
But truth is, I can't bear it -
that was sarcasm before.

Maybe it's unfair of me to caricature the pseudo-interest that I've often encountered, and Christians can sometimes be blamed for over-stating the unkindness of non-believers towards them. So often, religious enquiry is genuine, of course, and even when its motives are mixed, it deserves to be taken seriously.

The final verse of the poem touches on the sad reality that so many in our culture would rather not have a conversation about God at all, preferring instead to discuss the weather, or anything else, however trivial. We are fortunate, though, to be living in an age of relative political and religious freedom, where we're able to ask questions and to research the claims of Christianity without fear of arrest, even if our freedom of curiosity can sometimes be hemmed in by loud and insistent voices.

And pray for us, too, that God may open a door for our message, so that we may proclaim the mystery of Christ, for which I am in chains. Pray that I may proclaim it clearly, as I should. Be wise in the way you act toward outsiders; make the most of every opportunity. Let your conversation be always full of grace, seasoned with salt, so that you may know how to answer everyone.
(Colossians 4:3-6)

TEMPLE PRESENCE

Where Presence filled each sight and sound
With harmony and life,
And one who, fashioned from the ground,
Delighted in his wife;
Where grace and kindness filled their days
And goodness charged the air,
As all creation joined in praise
To Him who'd set it there –

To Him, who walked the very space,
Who knew and loved his own,
Where they could gaze upon his face
And wouldn't feel alone.
The One who spoke as loving friend,
Who shared his perfect will,
Was pleased to dwell where all was well
And everything was still.

Then all was lost to pride and death
And sickness, lies and shame;
The very ones he'd given breath
Now trembled at his name.
And fear and hate and hate and fear
Would hold the nations bound
To lifeless idols, sword and spear,
And blood upon the ground.

If love with love could be revealed
And life with life remade,
And broken, hurting souls were healed
And all the price was paid;
And those forgiven could forgive,
And angry hearts could mourn,
And if the dead began to live
Because a veil was torn –

See there, outside an ancient gate,
Mocked with a thorny crown,
One nailed and speared by human hate
For heaven's love come down –
There, where all the darkest powers
Had gathered to subdue,
To curse and crush in those few hours,
All that was good and true.

Unwanted, this unblemished lamb
Bore mocking and derision,
Where once the son of Abraham
Was spared through God's provision.
This mountain top, this place of meeting;
Sacrifice for all;
Sin condemned, at last completing
Judgement for the Fall.

Raised up, ruling from his throne,
And hidden from our sight,
He has become the cornerstone
Where love and faith unite.
We meet him, gathered or alone,
And in that holy place
New mercies fall upon his own,
And overwhelming grace.

Our Living Hope! When all concludes,
And at the trumpet's sound,
He'll stand among the multitudes
Upon untainted ground;
His own, from every tribe and tongue,
Raised up before their Lord,
And harmonies of "Worthy" sung,
And all the earth restored.

There's a wonderful symmetry between the beginning of Genesis and the end of Revelation. *Temple Presence* was written as a part of my reflection on the closeness of God's relationship with the man and woman in Genesis 2, and how that closeness is restored to us by the sacrificial ministry of Jesus, the ultimate temple. The Bible looks forward to when the world will be remade to become fully as God created it to be: "untainted ground", with death and evil forever banished from it – a world of restored relationship, and another marriage too, this time between Jesus and his bride, the community of believers worldwide, and through all time.

The presence of God is found in the tabernacle in the desert, in Solomon's temple in Jerusalem and many other places besides, but these meeting places are themselves representations of what had once been known before the fall, and always looking forward to a fuller and more universal revelation of God's glory in the world.

Of course, as a believer in Jesus these themes are central to my own life, since God's involvement in it – his presence today with any believer – could only have been made possible by his sacrificial giving of himself on the cross. It was here that he showed his enormous commitment to the world, and his tremendous love for humanity.

The kingdom of the world has become the kingdom of our Lord and his Messiah, and he will reign for ever and ever. (Revelation 11:15)

A VIEW OF THE KINGDOM

Suppose that I could make a call
To organise a viewing
Of resurrection life, and all
The things the raised are doing;
Perhaps a tour of what's in store,
With chat along the way
Of what the people felt and saw
On resurrection day.

And how they live and laugh and share
In all the soothing light
And unpolluted love that's there,
And unreserved delight.
And I would fall before the throne
Where songs and praises ring,
And maybe, feebly, add my own
To glorify the King.

All this is but a whim, of course,
I don't expect a view;
Eternal doors are closed to tours
And visitors are few.
Since all the power and glory there,
The splendour of his Name
And sweetness of his loving care,
Was shown us when he came.

The hope I've known is this alone:
That Jesus made a way,
And I, through goodness not my own,
Will see him, come the day.
His life among us here became
The grounds for all renewing;
He meets us in his cross and shame,
So never mind the viewing!

A View of the Kingdom continues the theme of God's remade earth, this time imagining a guided tour. The tone of the poem is light-hearted, but the suffering endured by Jesus, the final verse reminds us, was not trivial. Our interest in him should not be detached, as though we were casual tourists, but fully invested through well-founded faith.

The apostle Paul suggests that we have a wonderful "maturity" to look forward to, and that any ideas about our eternity that we might entertain in this life will inevitably be limited – just as no child really understands the complexities of the adult world. One day, all our imaginings of what the presence of God might be like will seem as nothing, compared to the actual splendour, beauty and glory that we encounter.

For we know in part and we prophesy in part, but when completeness comes, what is in part disappears. When I was a child, I talked like a child, I thought like a child, I reasoned like a child. When I became a man, I put the ways of childhood behind me. For now we see only a reflection as in a mirror; then we shall see face to face. Now I know in part; then I shall know fully, even as I am fully known. And now these three remain: faith, hope and love. But the greatest of these is love.
(1 Corinthians 13:9-13)

AN OLD MAN'S DESPAIR IN LOCKDOWN

Stripped of everything I truly cared for,
Denied sight of those I'd thought my own,
I pondered self-destructive schemes, alone,
As though emptiness was all that I'd been spared for.

I bemoaned my solitude, my loss, my pain,
As one shunned and left outside to rot,
Remembering, while all the world forgot,
The man I'd been, and couldn't be again.

I took a bible – long neglected and unread –
To find a psalm remembered from my youth;
Perturbed by sudden unfamiliar truth,
Tame organ chords fell silent in my head.

It cast light on my self-sufficient pride –
The dangerous quicksand of where I stood:
Bluster wouldn't offer hope – it never could,
And, blaming God, my faith had all but died.

I will bless his name, from now and to my last,
I'll honour him as all of heaven sings –
Take refuge in the shadow of his wings,
Till every trial and impulse for denial is past.

❧ @ ❧

Here a man is imagined with the story of Job in mind, driven almost to suicide by his loneliness and loss. Such despair has not been unusual over the past few years, where the trials of old age have been compounded by so many others. The story of Job offers hope, even to those whose losses are the greatest during such times. It speaks of deciding, in the face of total personal calamity, to acknowledge the complete goodness of God.

The old man in this poem is unexpectedly challenged as he revisits a psalm, particularly by the lines,

"I will take refuge in the shadow of your wings until the disaster has passed." (Ps. 57:1)

So often, it is in the encounter of verses such as these that we are prompted to review our lives and priorities. For this old man, as for many I've known who share a similar story, what had previously been mere religion, with no real answer to his overwhelming sadness, becomes a real relationship of trust and hope in God.

Have mercy on me, my God, have mercy on me,
for in you I take refuge.
I will take refuge in the shadow of your wings
until the disaster has passed.
I cry out to God Most High,
to God, who vindicates me.
He sends from heaven and saves me,
rebuking those who hotly pursue me—
God sends forth his love and his faithfulness.

I will praise you, Lord, among the nations;
    I will sing of you among the peoples.
For great is your love, reaching to the heavens;
    your faithfulness reaches to the skies.
Be exalted, O God, above the heavens;
    let your glory be over all the earth.
(Psalm 57:1-3; 9-11)

Bible Characters and Incidents
(Old Testament)

WHEN WE MET RAHAB

At Jericho's gate we were ordered to wait
While the guards asked us questions
and searched us for arms,
For their fine city state would only stay great
Through their vigilance, violence
and soldierly charms.

But they'd failed to discern we were Israelite spies,
Our mission: to see if we'd beat them in war;
But we asked our new friends if they might advise
On our finding a bed for the night - or a floor?

A sergeant approached, for a guard he was small,
With menacing eyes and an oversized gut,
"Rahab will take you both, pay her a call –
Then you'll have your pleasure, and we'll take our cut."

He turned to his friends, and together they laughed,
"I think you'll like Rahab – she lives by the wall,
And she lives by her favours, adept at her craft:
The finest in Jericho – open to all!"

So we went to find Rahab, upstairs from the gate,
And she came to the door in her slippers and gown,
And she told us she'd charge us a reasonable rate,
But we said we just needed a place to bed down.

"I took you both for good men", she replied,
"I'm tired of those creeps", with a sigh and a frown;
"The Lord is with you, it can't be denied,
And he must be against this idolatrous town!"

"They've done nothing but use me and cast me aside,
They laugh at me, taunt me, exploit and abuse –
But you've been respectful, kind, dignified,
Quick to affirm me, and slow to accuse."

She told us she knew we'd been sent by the Lord,
How they spoke of our conquests, the parted Red Sea;
"All Jericho trembles, for fire and sword
Will soon overwhelm us, my people and me."

The King's men arrived,
but she'd hidden us from sight,
(We slept on the roof, beneath stalks of flax);
Told them we'd left town while it was light –
If they hurried off now, they might pick up our tracks!

She woke us, and said she could help us escape;
Gates locked, we could hear the frantic guards call,
"You're not the first men that I've seen in a scrape",
And she lowered a rope from her room on the wall.

Before we climbed down, she said "Promise one thing,
That you'll remember this friendship I've shown;
When your armies invade us and unseat our king,
Leave me and my family untouched in my home."

"You and yours will not die by the sword,"
We said reassuringly, scrambling through,
"Just fix to this window a scarlet-dyed chord:
When they see it, our people will know that it's you."

We climbed down the rope and escaped to the heights
(With provisions and blankets
from Rahab's own store);
We hid under rocks for three days and three nights
Before braving the highway again, on day four.

Returning to camp we found Joshua's tent
And we told him of Rahab, and Canaanite dread
That the Israelites conquered wherever they went;
Our God fought for us: the message had spread.

For Rahab, he promised the greatest reward
For her faithfulness, boldness and generous supplies,
He'd watch for the window with scarlet dyed chord,
Giving thanks for this lady who'd sheltered his spies.

When We Met Rahab takes the account of the two spies in Joshua ch.2, putting their story into their own mouths. I wanted to explore Rahab's motivations for helping them, and the reasons for her solid faith, in the most idolatrous of cities, in Israel's God. The tale of her bravery is a Sunday school staple, but the guards at the city gate are my own addition to the story. Soldiers do appear in the Bible's account, but there is nothing in the passage to suggest that Rahab was being pimped by them. Nonetheless, we can confidently assume that as a prostitute she would have been familiar with the most unsavoury aspects of city life, seen men at their worst, and, along with the other womenfolk of Jericho, would likely have lived in constant fear of violence and abuse at their hands.

The point of this story, and of the subsequent fall of Jericho, is to say that among the various deities of the ancient near east, just as in the world today, there was only one true creator God – the God revealed to Moses and the Israelites in the wilderness. The Canaanites had become dehumanised *because* of their religion, not in spite of it. They may have been fearful of this conquering people and their God, yet they were unwilling to turn away from their idolatry. Rahab, alone among them all, courageously took a stand on the right side of history.

Israel's God would one day reveal himself in the person of Jesus. Interestingly, Matthew's Gospel mentions Rahab among his ancestors, one of four gentile women in his genealogy (Matt. Ch.1) who married into the Israelite tribe of Judah, and into the line of David. Immoral though her life had been, Rahab was rescued and restored on account of her faith in the goodness and supremacy of the true God, even taking a crucial part in history as one of Jesus's forebears. As so often in the Bible, this story of hope and restoration in one person, through Jesus becomes our own story, and ultimately the story of all of creation.

Before the spies lay down for the night, she went up on the roof and said to them, "I know that the LORD has given you this land and that a great fear of you has fallen on us, so that all who live in this country are melting in fear because of you. We have heard how the LORD dried up the water of the Red Sea for you when you came out of Egypt, and what you did to Sihon and Og, the two kings of the Amorites east of the Jordan, whom you completely destroyed. When we heard of it, our hearts melted in fear and everyone's courage failed because of you, for the LORD your God is God in heaven above and on the earth below..."
(Joshua 2:8-11)

APPROACHES TO THE STORY OF
THE WIDOW OF ZAREPHATH

A starving widow with her son;
A prophet asks for food:
There's something there for everyone;
It's godly, or it's rude.
And oil flows but no one knows
why *she* received such grace,
But that she reaps just as she sows,
regardless of her race.

A rogue would highlight *blessing*
in the gifting of her meal;
New oil and oats all stressing
rich returns from such a deal.
But others see her playing the host
as evidence of trust
In everything she valued most:
that Israel's God *is* just.

God knew she'd faithfully comply,
a Calvinist would say,
For he'd ordained the widow's cry,
and her redemption day.
Faith alone, and grace alone
would be this sermon's theme,
A sombre, self-abasing tone,
and nothing too extreme.

But what of those who take the view,
"She's righteous for her deeds"?
Pelagian – it's nothing new,
and dangerous where it leads.
The Gnostic would deny her strife,
and say she wasn't frightened,
Since "carelessness of fleshly life"
means "all the more enlightened".

A feminist might stand aghast –
this shameless, greedy man!
Such chauvinism, unsurpassed,
demands the Bible's ban!
And Communists would be dismayed:
the oatcake wasn't shared;
Production brazenly displayed,
and none of it declared!

For others still, the story's core
screams urgent words of caution:
Who would make their oven roar
to bake a single portion?
A meagre cake, no matter whose,
consumed in just a bite!
Surely, no one would excuse
the fuel they burned that night.

Jesus comments on the scene,
on where God sent his servant;
With Israel's widows, like their queen,
uncaring, unobservant,
Sidon's widow, poor and weak,
showed love with godly flavour,
And faith apparently unique,
by which she found his favour.

ᴏ᷒ᴗᴗᴗᴗ @ ᴗᴗᴗᴗᴗ

It's a common complaint that Bible passages can be used to support whatever point of view a preacher wishes to promote. This particular story about the widow of Zarephath is spoken of by Jesus himself in Luke Ch. 4, which perhaps makes sound comment on the passage more likely. But even so, I wanted to explore (in a light-hearted fashion) some of the ways in which it could be abused.

I begin with the "rogue" who would preach the message of prosperity: "Just give and give (especially your money – to us) and God will multiply his blessings to you". This message certainly isn't what this passage teaches, and it's not the message of the true church, either. We are asked simply to give, with no consideration of whether any material gain to ourselves may come of it. The widow's sacrificial generosity was born out of her trust in the character of God, and her regard for him.

My dig at Calvinist teaching is not to say that it's wrong, but only that I think it can sometimes be blinkered, perhaps seeing the world as if through arrow loops set into the various thick walls it defends.

False teachings of "salvation by works", and of Gnostic "enlightenment", both evident in churches and in popular thought today, have dogged Christian witness for many hundreds of years, so I include them here with their respective misinterpretations of the widow's story.

Finally, the God of the Bible holds out his loving arms to Marxists, feminists and environmentalists alike, but ultimately his message of hope and peace is not theirs. I include them here only to comment upon how the "isms" of our own day can often set themselves up in opposition to a true knowledge of God, much as Baal worship did in Elijah's time.

Some time later the brook dried up because there had been no rain in the land. Then the word of the LORD came to him: "Go at once to Zarephath in the region of Sidon and stay there. I have directed a widow there to supply you with food." So he went to Zarephath. When he came to the town gate, a widow was there gathering sticks. He called to her and asked, "Would you bring me a little water in a jar so I may have a drink?" As she was going to get it, he called, "And bring me, please, a piece of bread."

"As surely as the LORD your God lives," she replied, "I don't have any bread—only a handful of flour in a jar and a little olive oil in a jug. I am gathering a few sticks to take home and make a meal for myself and my son, that we may eat it—and die."

Elijah said to her, "Don't be afraid. Go home and do as you have said. But first make a small loaf of bread for me from what you have and bring it to me, and then make something for yourself and your son. For this is what the LORD, the God of Israel, says: 'The jar of flour will not be used up and the jug of oil will not run dry until the day the LORD sends rain on the land.'"

She went away and did as Elijah had told her. So there was food every day for Elijah and for the woman and her family. For the jar of flour was not used up and the jug of oil did not run dry, in keeping with the word of the LORD spoken by Elijah.

(1 Kings 17:7-16)

BROTHER, WE ARE DYING

Brother, we are dying; could you spare
A little oatmeal and some oil from your store?
Sister, look, it's not that we don't care,
But you'd only keep on coming back for more.

I might have fed you both a year ago,
But shortage puts us all in prudent mood;
And now my own reserves are running low,
I find it hard to give away my food.

Is it beyond your neighbours in your street,
To lend a bowl of oil, a cup of flour?
Don't the temples offer things to eat?
And didn't you save coins against this hour?

I had some money saved, but now I've spent it;
My neighbours helped to feed us while they could –
Kind at first, they started to resent it,
And when the giving stopped, we understood.

I could have sold myself to men, it's true;
And worked at Sidon's temple with the rest,
But now I'm weak, and I have come to you,
And we'll return home, just as you suggest.

* * * * * * * * * *

What's to lose from this man's sudden visit?
One final act of service while I live?
It's hardly going to change our fortunes, is it?
This single oaten cake I have to give.

While the first of these poems about the widow of Zarephath was an exploration of what lessons we might (and might not) draw from her story, in this second poem I wanted to consider some of the excuses we might satisfy ourselves with to withhold our generosity. The scene is invented for the sake of the poem; the Bible speaks of no such encounter, nor of any brother that she might have visited for support.

Even so, we do know of her meeting with Elijah, and of her desperation at that point, for herself and her son.

Janice Joplin sang, "Freedom's just another word for 'nothin' left to lose'". Such may be the case for many who come to Christian faith only after reaching rock bottom in their lives, and perhaps there's an element of it in the widow's thinking, in the moment, as she selflessly gives all she has. Nonetheless, it seems to me that this widow gave of herself naturally and willingly, mainly because it was in her nature to recognise Israel's God. I think she had been practising faith and selfless giving in a harsh world long before she ever met Elijah the prophet.

*In your relationships with one another, have the same
mindset as Christ Jesus:
Who, being in very nature God,
did not consider equality with God something to be
used to his own advantage;
rather, he made himself nothing
by taking the very nature of a servant,
being made in human likeness.
And being found in appearance as a man,
he humbled himself
by becoming obedient to death—
even death on a cross!
Therefore God exalted him to the highest place
and gave him the name that is above every name,
that at the name of Jesus every knee should bow,
in heaven and on earth and under the earth,
and every tongue acknowledge that Jesus Christ is Lord,
to the glory of God the Father.*
(Philippians 2: 5-11)

EZEKIEL'S COMMISSION (EZEK. 2-3)

God told Ezekiel the prophet
To read from a scroll, and then scoff it;
He warned that the Jews
Wouldn't welcome his news,
That they'd scorn him, but not put him off it.

The words in his stomach sat queasy
For he knew that his task wasn't easy;
The people were hard
And as slippery as lard,
Idolatrous, prideful and sleazy.

God, knowing the hardness of men,
Encouraged Ezekiel again,
He strengthened and raised him
Through voices that praised him
And all of his glory, Amen.

Ezekiel rose to his feet
And he ate what God gave him to eat;
Through all of his testing
He'd always find rest in
God's faithfulness - heavenly sweet.

Ezekiel's ministry to the people of Judah was never going to meet with "success" in human terms, except that he would remain faithful, himself, to the God who called him. The Babylonians had already come and would come again; Jerusalem's walls would be reduced to rubble, the temple would be destroyed, and another generation of people would suffer Babylonian brutality and exile. His plea that his people turn back to God was a forlorn hope from the start. Even so, the book of Ezekiel is ultimately a prophesy of God's good purposes for his people and the world, as one day, God's presence would return to the land, and to the city. This is fulfilled in the coming of Messiah, who spoke of himself as the very presence of God on Earth.

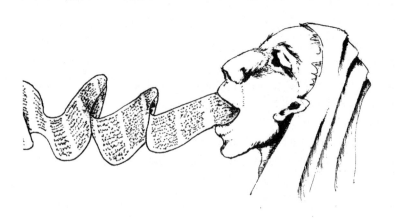

He said to me, "Son of man, stand up on your feet and I will speak to you." As he spoke, the Spirit came into me and raised me to my feet, and I heard him speaking to me. He said: "Son of man, I am sending you to the Israelites, to a rebellious nation that has rebelled against me; they and their ancestors have been in revolt against me to this very day.

[....]

And you, son of man, do not be afraid of them or their words. Do not be afraid, though briers and thorns are all around you and you live among scorpions. Do not be afraid of what they say or be terrified by them, though they are a rebellious people. You must speak my words to them, whether they listen or fail to listen, for they are rebellious. But you, son of man, listen to what I say to you. Do not rebel like that rebellious people; open your mouth and eat what I give you."

Then I looked, and I saw a hand stretched out to me. In it was a scroll, which he unrolled before me. On both sides of it were written words of lament and mourning and woe. And he said to me, "Son of man, eat what is before you, eat this scroll; then go and speak to the people of Israel." So I opened my mouth, and he gave me the scroll to eat. Then he said to me, "Son of man, eat this scroll I am giving you and fill your stomach with it." So I ate it, and it tasted as sweet as honey in my mouth.

(Ezekiel 2:1 – 3:3)

Bible Characters and Incidents
(New Testament)

SURVIVING CHRISTMAS

Bent under foreign rule,
cracked voices of seething discontent
Grieve loss and ridicule –
groans of loud, longing lament;
Milked, despoiled chosen race,
nations' light now burning low;
Sorrowful, stifling, the place;
hollow and pitiful the show.

A wild, risk-ridden scheme
in the soiled story of the earth;
One shrill maternal scream,
and Life, flop-floundered in human birth.
Regiments of ruin crave for death
as angels guard him there;
And his first, gasping breath:
dust; smoke; cold, foul-stinking air.

Lines of battle drawn in those first raw,
momentous hours,
Against not blood and brawn,
but earth's dark deceiving powers –
Foiled; feeble to prevent
the dowsing of evil's sweep and spread!
Judean infant, heaven sent,
finally to crush the serpent's head.

Of all the births in all of human history, this was an especially messy and dangerous one. Jesus was born into particularly brutal times, as the province of Judaea suffered under the yoke of Roman rule. But while the humiliated nation mourned their losses, they also hoped for God's promised salvation. It was a time of expectation, of prophetic fulfilment. *Surviving Christmas* is my attempt to place the birth of Jesus within its grim context.

Our Christmas carols remind us how Jesus was celebrated and worshiped by the hosts of heaven at his birth, but those same hosts also guarded him from the spiritual powers that wanted him dead. He survived childhood and early adulthood under the same protection, until the day when it was finally, agonisingly withheld. Through his death on the cross he would break those same destructive powers forever.

As we live by faith in Jesus, we have every reason to celebrate – especially at Christmas time. But we also find ourselves engaged in the same conflict against the unseen dark powers Jesus faced. More than we know, perhaps, we are preserved and protected by the hosts of heaven, and by the presence of God with us.

Dark forces we meet with today oppose the witness, fellowship and growth of believers within the church, and foul the world around us with deceit and resentment, corruption and death. But we can know with confidence that they are a defeated enemy. A stricken ship, spine broken and taking on water, cannot stay afloat for very long before it's pulled down beneath the waves.

The Son is the image of the invisible God, the firstborn over all creation. For in him all things were created: things in heaven and on earth, visible and invisible, whether thrones or powers or rulers or authorities; all things have been created through him and for him. He is before all things, and in him all things hold together.
(Colossians 1:15-17)

JOSEPH'S STORY

It seems a funny thing to me
That such a simple family
And such a simple man as I –
And I have often questioned why –
Should be the ones to teach a Saviour
Gentle thoughts and good behaviour.

Right from my early childhood
I'd learned my trade – I work with wood.
My father taught me; and one day,
He stopped me in my work to say,
"My son, about your time of life
You need to think about a wife,"

"For you are now a spritely teen,
Stout and held in good esteem";
They'd talk about the girls they knew
From Nazareth's synagogue, and who
They thought would suit me best to wed,
And finally, this is what they said:

"Joseph, we know the girl for you,
She's godly, and she's pretty too,
It's Mary, sweet in all her ways,
She's sure to bring you happy days!"
Our families met and all agreed
That she could be the wife I'd need.

So we were promised from that day,
Each to the other, come what may.
And what delight! And oh! The joy!
For I was now the promised boy!
And when the clans could meet, they said,
They'd hold a feast, and we'd be wed.

But then one dreadful day she came
To tell us she was not to blame;
To say it was God's child she carried,
Even though she wasn't married;
The angel's words, she said, were clear,
And she and I were not to fear.

But I was angry at the shame
She'd brought upon her family name,
And hurt that she'd dishonoured mine –
And shocked she'd claimed it all divine!
Defiled and used beneath another;
Wicked tales! Unholy mother!

I feared she was in mortal danger
Having entertained a stranger;
But if I'd publicly disowned her
They'd have all come round and stoned her.
So I resolved to pull the plug
And sweep it all beneath the rug.

I now remember this with grief
And I regret my unbelief,
For as I slept upon my bed
An angel came to me and said,
"Now Joseph, all she said was true,
She never broke her troth to you."

"And now you know, you have to take her–
Honour her and please your maker;
No more than you is she a sinner:
God has set this child within her;
Rest assured, she is no liar –
She *is* the mother to Messiah."

"And you're to treat him as your own
And raise him in your family home;
Dote on him as a loving dad,
Train him to be a godly lad.
You'll call him Jesus for his name,
To tell the world a Saviour came."

So God assured *us*, as *we'd* heard,
But all round Galilee was word
Of Mary's sin, and even mine –
I hoped it all would pass with time;
But ever since, we've had to bear
The daily jibe, the judging stare.

And cruel laughter, shame and doubt
Have followed Jesus all about,
But still he laughs and loves and grows,
And says God helps him in his woes.
If he can bear it, so can we,
And through our boy God blesses me.

I often think about the night
The angel came to put me right,
And what a cruel judge I'd been
To speak of things I hadn't seen;
To think the worst, proclaim the crime,
When all the while, the sin was mine!

I'll gladly bear the mockers' pain
But let me never judge again!
And so I know, without a doubt,
That God will work his purpose out
To heal the nations through my boy –
To bring salvation, peace and joy.

I imagine a young Joseph here, and his family life around the time of his betrothal to Mary. Our tradition has him as a carpenter, but his skills may have been more general, as a builder, rather than exclusively working with wood – a scarce and expensive commodity in ancient Galilee. I have him reflecting on his mistrust of Mary's story, which in truth was understandable by anyone's standard.

It took an angel's visit for Joseph to recognise his error, and I wonder how many humanly understandable doubts and suspicions we harbour of each other, or of God, that could impede the working of his Spirit in our lives, families, or church communities. It is through moments of trust and faith that we grow, and I have no doubt that for Joseph's life this was an exceptional time of growth as he learned to appreciate God's hand in the seemingly hopeless and dangerous situations he encountered.

This is how the birth of Jesus the Messiah came about: His mother Mary was pledged to be married to Joseph, but before they came together, she was found to be pregnant through the Holy Spirit. Because Joseph her husband was faithful to the law, and yet did not want to expose her to public disgrace, he had in mind to divorce her quietly. But after he had considered this, an angel of the Lord appeared to him in a dream and said, "Joseph son of

David, do not be afraid to take Mary home as your wife,
because what is conceived in her is from the Holy
Spirit. She will give birth to a son, and you are to give him
the name Jesus, because he will save his people from their
sins."
All this took place to fulfill what the Lord had said
through the prophet: "The virgin will conceive and give
birth to a son, and they will call him Immanuel" (which
means "God with us").
When Joseph woke up, he did what the angel of the Lord
had commanded him and took Mary home as his
wife. But he did not consummate their marriage until she
gave birth to a son. And he gave him the name Jesus.
(Matthew 1:18-25)

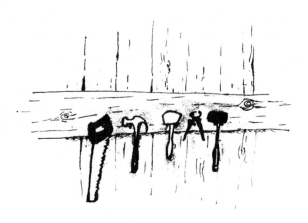

WHEN THE WOMAN OF SYCHAR
CALLED THE SAMARITANS

Five times divorced, you say? Well, well!
Damaged goods? Oh, that's a little mean –
Cruel tales that heartless neighbours tell,
Who love to think themselves so pure and clean!

Your grudging kinsman's prison without bars,
Unforgiving as the mid-day sun;
The daily grind, the gruelling water jars
Your punishment for having mothered none?

Perhaps a man could help you to conceive
Of being loved, and not just for your womb,
And defy those superstitions you believe –
Accusing clouds of fetid, toxic gloom.

A man who'd bring the hope of fuller life,
With words so true, so cleansing, fresh and free,
That being his, though neither mum nor wife,
You're wholly you, as you were made to be.

∼⊙∼

The "woman at the well", whose name we aren't told by John the gospel writer, was given the honour of being among the first to make Jesus known in Samaria, inaugurating his ministry beyond Judea, to the whole world. She would not have seen herself as particularly worthy of such a crucial role in God's scheme. She didn't count herself as being worth very much at all.

My poem imagines her in a phone conversation with the Samaritans (a modern charity of volunteers who listen on the phone to those suffering extreme mental stress, or contemplating suicide), although, of course, a trained counsellor would probably have listened more, and said less. It's a bad pun, but this lady did, in fact, call the Samaritans (her own people) to come to know Jesus.

What had persuaded her? This woman felt worthless among her own people. Many today take the sympathetic view that she was a woman discarded by successive husbands due to her inability to bear children. Thus rejected, it's suggested that she now lived with a kinsman, grudgingly kept by him as tradition demanded.

Whatever her story, Jesus treated her with dignity – perhaps the first person in a while to speak kindly to her, listening, but seeing behind her words the terrible confusion and superstition of her culture, and all that it had cost her in her life. Her perceived "failure" to bear a child, seen even as a curse, would have dictated all her social interactions within the household, and in the community – even to the point of her having to collect water alone, during the hottest time of the day.

What Jesus offered her was a radically different view of herself, her community, and her calling, but most of all, a radically new understanding of what it means for God to dwell amongst people. She learned that true religion was life-giving and purposeful, when all she had ever known were the stifling and oppressive traditions born out of distorted impressions of God.

Jesus may not have healed her with the family life she'd never had, but he gave her a new vision of her own value in God's sight, and a new purpose for her life, as an ambassador for him.

Jesus answered, "Everyone who drinks this water will be thirsty again, but whoever drinks the water I give them will never thirst. Indeed, the water I give them will become in them a spring of water welling up to eternal life."
The woman said to him, "Sir, give me this water so that I won't get thirsty and have to keep coming here to draw water."
He told her, "Go, call your husband and come back."
"I have no husband," she replied.

Jesus said to her, "You are right when you say you have no husband. The fact is, you have had five husbands, and the man you now have is not your husband. What you have just said is quite true." [...]

The woman said, "I know that Messiah" (called Christ) "is coming. When he comes, he will explain everything to us." Then Jesus declared, "I, the one speaking to you—I am he." Just then his disciples returned and were surprised to find him talking with a woman. But no one asked, "What do you want?" or "Why are you talking with her?"

Then, leaving her water jar, the woman went back to the town and said to the people, "Come, see a man who told me everything I ever did. Could this be the Messiah?" They came out of the town and made their way toward him.

(John 4:13-30)

MY ROCK

My rock was further down the shore,
A cove where none could see,
Along a path that no one took,
No one but me.
I'd scrub my clothes with loud lament,
Beat, pray and cry
That I'd be spared this suffering,
That I might die.

My rock of grief and was all I had,
I'd long since spent my gold;
My property for costly balms,
Had all been sold.
And bloodied rags adorned my rock
Like cuts of drying meat,
Dripping brief, pink-tinted clouds
About my feet.

But on the day the Teacher came,
I jostled close, unseen,
Only to touch his tasselled shawl
And I'd be clean.
And as I let my shaking hand
Brush down upon his cloak,
Such healing flowed and warmed my soul!
But then he spoke –

Who touched me?" as he turned to me,
"Who was it of you here?"
I met the one that I'd defiled,
Filled with fear.
His voice, all calm and tenderness:
"Daughter, quiet your soul,
Your faith has healed you of your ills,
And you are whole."

I'm thankful that he took from me
My shame, my bloodied past;
I know *him* for the better rock,
And live, at last.

The gospel stories speak of sickness, poverty, suffering, bereavement, insanity and social exclusion, all as things that Jesus encountered regularly in the course of his ministry. He had truly entered a broken world, and in the woman he meets in John 11, many levels of brokenness are evident.

She is known to us as "the woman with the issue of blood", and her brief mention in the gospels comes sandwiched within another story of Jesus responding to a request to heal the daughter of Jairus, a synagogue leader. He eventually raises this little girl from the dead.

My poem introduces the woman washing her clothes, and especially her rags, which the bible makes no mention of, but which must have been a regular task for her in her lonely life. Living in poverty, ostracised by her community, considered cursed and ritually unclean, she was everything that Jairus's daughter wasn't. She would have died long before her time, as the little girl did, but likely unnoticed and un-mourned. Nonetheless, she seized upon a chance to connect with Jesus

- unannounced, of course, and hoping not to be seen in the crowd.

Jesus calls attention to her, though, not to rebuke or shame her, but to honour her; to call her "daughter", and to assure her that her faith in him had not been misplaced. Whatever reasons we may have to reach out for Jesus, it will always be met with the same kindness, and the same willingness to dignify our lives.

We may not experience physical healing as this lady did, when our ailments seem beyond the ability of doctors to cure (though some people do), but a touch from him can reset our thoughts and emotions, and give us an entirely new understanding of who God has made us to be, and how we might then see ourselves, in relation to him and to those around us.

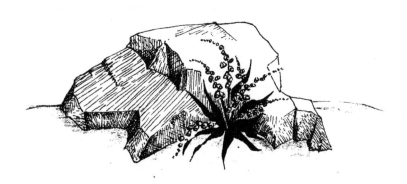

*And a woman was there who had been subject to
bleeding for twelve years. She had suffered a great deal
under the care of many doctors and had spent all she had,
yet instead of getting better she grew worse. When she
heard about Jesus, she came up behind him in the crowd
and touched his cloak, because she thought, "If I just touch
his clothes, I will be healed." Immediately her bleeding
stopped and she felt in her body that she was freed from
her suffering.*

*At once Jesus realized that power had gone out from him.
He turned around in the crowd and asked, "Who touched
my clothes?"*

*"You see the people crowding against you," his disciples
answered, "and yet you can ask, 'Who touched me?'"*

*But Jesus kept looking around to see who had done
it. Then the woman, knowing what had happened to her,
came and fell at his feet and, trembling with fear, told him
the whole truth. He said to her, "Daughter, your faith has
healed you. Go in peace and be freed from your suffering."*
(Mark 5:25-34)

WHEN LAZARUS DIED

He was sick, so sick, and you knew,
And we begged him to hold on for you;
We all waited, and prayed
That you'd not be delayed;
That the message we'd sent had got through.

But he died. And you didn't show;
Lord why was your journey so slow?
This lingering response –
Was it nonchalance,
In the time that it took you to go?

Some friend, who doesn't drop all
To attend to the dying man's call!
To profess that you care,
When you couldn't be there,
Seems not to be friendship at all.

. . . .

No, this is not how it ends;
He's laid down his life for his friends!
And he's broken death's power,
No matter the hour,
And whatever the darkness pretends.

It's not uncommon for those who have experienced loss to question whether Jesus cares, and to ask why God has allowed the death of a loved one. Mary and Martha were baffled by Jesus's delay, both separately greeting him with the words, "Lord, if you had been here my brother would not have died", while John records others among the mourners saying, "Could not he who opened the eyes of the blind man have kept this man from dying?"

Lazarus was raised from the dead, however, in a demonstration of God's broader purpose in resurrection, through Jesus. He says to Martha, "I am the resurrection and the life. The one who believes in me will live, even though they die; and whoever lives by believing in me will never die. Do you believe this?"

Martha stated her belief in Jesus as the promised Messiah, but this passage invites us, as readers, to examine our own level of faith in him.

My final verse speaks of Christ's victory over death, but also of how blinded we can be to it. In their grief, Mary and Martha both needed reminding of his total authority, and creative and restorative power. It is often in our own times of grief and despondency that we find our hope as believers beginning to fog. Those are the times when a testimony like Martha's can have extraordinary power, not just in lifting our own spirits, but in affecting the lives of those around us:

"I believe that you are the Messiah, the Son of God, who is to come into the world."

On his arrival, Jesus found that Lazarus had already been in the tomb for four days. Now Bethany was less than two miles from Jerusalem, and many Jews had come to Martha and Mary to comfort them in the loss of their brother. When Martha heard that Jesus was coming, she went out to meet him, but Mary stayed at home.

"Lord," Martha said to Jesus, "if you had been here, my brother would not have died. But I know that even now God will give you whatever you ask."

Jesus said to her, "Your brother will rise again."

Martha answered, "I know he will rise again in the resurrection at the last day."

Jesus said to her, "I am the resurrection and the life. The one who believes in me will live, even though they die; and whoever lives by believing in me will never die. Do you believe this?"

"Yes, Lord," she replied, "I believe that you are the Messiah, the Son of God, who is to come into the world."
[…]

So they took away the stone. Then Jesus looked up and said, "Father, I thank you that you have heard me. I knew that you always hear me, but I said this for the benefit of the people standing here, that they may believe that you sent me."

When he had said this, Jesus called in a loud voice, "Lazarus, come out!" The dead man came out, his hands and feet wrapped with strips of linen, and a cloth around his face. Jesus said to them, "Take off the grave clothes and let him go."
(John 11:17-27; 41-44)

MAUNDY THURSDAY

Preparation.
We took a room above a busy street;
Pilgrims passed, pressed,
pushed for lodgings for the feast,
But God provided ours –
Our God

Twelve reclined
About the tables; bowls, cups and platters spread,
Minds racing, Kingdom hopes,
and how the prophets said
God would provide for us –
Our God

Our Teacher,
Stooping low, a towel about his waist,
Washed, rubbed, dried our feet,
no matter the confusion raised
Deep down inside for us,
Our God

Bread and wine,
Raised, blessed and passed around to each,
No call to arms; spent blood and body were to teach
and call to mind for us
Our God

Sunset on Thursday night marks the beginning of the day of Preparation in the Jewish week, before the Sabbath, which begins on Friday evening. Of course, it was a Passover meal that the disciples were to share together that night, an annual reminder of God's rescue of his people from captivity in Egypt.

The disciples would each have had their own ideas of how the Messiah was going to offer rescue to his people in their own day, while Judas had already given up on any hope he'd once had in Jesus. Just as they would not have expected their room to be available, they didn't expect their leader to wash anyone's feet that evening, nor that he would speak of his broken body and shed blood, as if he were himself the sacrificial Passover lamb. For all their teaching received during the three years of Jesus's ministry, this would have been a truly baffling sequence of events for the disciples - events and ideas that they were only really able to make sense of after the resurrection.

Many today would find the account of the Last Supper bewildering, and all the more so as our culture is so far removed from Jewish traditions. The significance of symbolic foods, and references to the Book of Exodus might all be lost on modern readers. But the first believers found themselves confronted, just a few days later, with the fact of a dead victim of Roman crucifixion standing again, fully alive in front of them. They were able to grasp the real meanings and purposes of Jesus's ministry only by working back from that encounter.

Our task remains the same as theirs, as we consider the implications for ourselves of a crucified man, completely returned to life nearly two thousand years ago, who spoke of himself as the embodiment of God's rescue for the whole of his creation – not just the Israel of Exodus – from the oppression of all the world's evils.

And he took bread, gave thanks and broke it, and gave it to them, saying, "This is my body given for you; do this in remembrance of me."
In the same way, after the supper he took the cup,
saying, "This cup is the new covenant in my blood, which is poured out for you…"
(Luke 22:19-20)

THE CENTURION

We led him out beyond the city gate
Onto the hill, where women wept for grief,
And mockers jeered and spat with studied hate;
We nailed him there, with either side a thief.

Our dismal task, on raising up the three,
To watch them writhe and die in hopeless pain;
But now a thief, bound fast against his tree,
Enrolled himself in this Messiah's reign.

The sun beat, merciless in that place of death,
Welding wounds to wood; scourged back
with torn skin
Glued, then prized away each laboured breath,
And still he turned his thorn-gouged head to him!

He spoke as one who knew him, one who cared,
And promised paradise with him that very day;
In shameful death he blessed! I stood and stared,
Seized by the power of what I'd heard him say:

Words of life! But I, Rome's servant sworn,
A lifeless soul, unmoved by death or pain:
That cold indifference died, and hope was born,
There on that hill and in this man we'd slain.

The soldiers at the foot of the cross responded fearfully to the ground shaking and various other supernatural events at Jesus's death. I think the centurion must also have been affected by Jesus throughout the day, as he prayed for his executioners' forgiveness, for example, and he surely would have heard him offer reassurance to the thief crucified beside him.

In the centurion's confession the temporal powers of Roman military rule collide with the true authority of the God of Israel. "Truly this was the son of God", he says, not of the Emperor Tiberius Caesar, but of the broken man whose whipping and crucifixion he had supervised.

The reach of the gospel into the centurion's life offers hope to the most hardened of us, to those traumatised or guilt-plagued by their own past, and especially to those most beholden to authorities and structures that stand in opposition to Jesus.

There was a written notice above him, which read: THIS IS THE KING OF THE JEWS.
One of the criminals who hung there hurled insults at him: "Aren't you the Messiah? Save yourself and us!"
But the other criminal rebuked him. "Don't you fear God," he said, "since you are under the same sentence? We are punished justly, for we are getting what our deeds deserve. But this man has done nothing wrong."
Then he said, "Jesus, remember me when you come into your kingdom."
Jesus answered him, "Truly I tell you, today you will be with me in paradise."
(Luke 23:38-43)

At noon, darkness came over the whole land until three in the afternoon. And at three in the afternoon Jesus cried out in a loud voice, "Eloi, Eloi, lema sabachthani?" (which means "My God, my God, why have you forsaken me?"). When some of those standing near heard this, they said, "Listen, he's calling Elijah."

Someone ran, filled a sponge with wine vinegar, put it on a staff, and offered it to Jesus to drink. "Now leave him alone. Let's see if Elijah comes to take him down," he said. With a loud cry, Jesus breathed his last.

The curtain of the temple was torn in two from top to bottom. And when the centurion, who stood there in front of Jesus, saw how he died, he said, "Surely this man was the Son of God!"

Some women were watching from a distance. Among them were Mary Magdalene, Mary the mother of James the younger and of Joseph, and Salome. In Galilee these women had followed him and cared for his needs. Many other women who had come up with him to Jerusalem were also there.

(Mark 15:33-40)

EMMAUS AND JERUSALEM

He joined us as we walked,
And he asked us as we talked
Why it was we seemed so burdened by the day,
And we wondered he'd not known
Of all the happenings in the town
That we related as we ambled on our way.

Then he said it was foretold
By all the prophets from of old
How Messiah was to die and rise again;
That all these things had passed,
And now the Promised One at last
Had come, and had been crucified by men.

But we shouldn't be forlorn,
As we had been since the dawn,
Now the "third day" that he'd talked about was here.
Oh, we'd heard the odd report –
All most unlikely, so we'd thought,
As our liberation hopes had turned to fear.

When we reached our place to stay
He made as if to turn away,
But we liked him and we wanted to learn more,
So he smiled, and stayed and shared
While our dinner was prepared,
Speaking further on the prophets and the law.

It was when he broke the bread,
After everything he'd said,
And we'd still not recognised that it was him,
And as he blessed the bread and passed it,
That was when we finally grasped it,
And why our hearts had seemed to burn within.

When he disappeared from view
We knew exactly what to do,
Though, when we told them back in town we thought
they'd doubt it;
But they knew it to be true
Because Peter saw him too,
And we spent some time in praise to God about it.

Jesus met with us there too,
From his greeting we all knew,
As he spoke transcendent peace into the room;
None doubted he was there,
And though it hadn't been our prayer,
We knew him living, breathing, risen from his tomb.

∼◦◦◦ @ ◦◦◦∼

There is something comical in the account of the two
disciples on the road to Emmaus. The despondent Cleopas
and his friend, so full of hope in Jesus before the arrest, but
now crushed by the events of Good Friday. Jesus, risen from
the dead, engages with their fears and disappointments and
explains their scriptures to them, all the while remaining
unrecognised until the moment of breaking bread at their
guest house that evening.

This is a story about the presence of God, in the person of
Jesus, among his people. Jesus had spoken to his disciples

about the sign of Jonah, but the gospels emphasise just how unprepared they were to witness his bodily appearance among them. And yet these encounters occurred, impacting the disciples so profoundly that they spoke and wrote of them to their dying days – most of them, of course, dying on account of their bearing witness to it.

Perhaps there are times when we, like these two disciples, are not able to grasp how close Jesus is to us, and instead allow despondency and disillusionment to gain a hold on our lives. The testimony of the disciples can help us, but the ongoing experiences of present-day believers, encountering the risen Jesus in all kinds of circumstances, can also be wonderfully encouraging.

I will sing of the LORD's great love forever;
with my mouth I will make your faithfulness known
through all generations.
I will declare that your love stands firm forever,
that you have established your faithfulness in heaven
itself.
(Psalm 89:1-2)

I'M SORRY ST BARTHOLOMEW

I'm sorry St Bartholomew,
for what your day became:
The memory of a slaughter
that forever bears your name;
Since all our days would tarnish,
were we to name them thus,
For their betrayals, hurts and evils,
by others and by us.

A Calvinist for a groom and a Catholic princess bride
In a unifying gesture that served only to divide,
But I'm sorry it's the thing we now associate with you:
The heaps of butchered Huguenots
in fifteen seventy-two.

Better if we'd call to mind your apostolic zeal,
Your life of faith and hardship
and your ministry to heal;
Your preaching of the gospel
to vagabond and lord,
The service and the sufferings
your biographers record.

You followed Jesus willingly,
and knew him as his friend,
And testified to loving him
until the bitter end;

Helpless as they bound you
and stripped you of your skin,
You knew the spite of hateful hearts,
the cruelty within.

But now another episode of treachery and blood
Has fixed your name in history,
and dragged it through the mud;
I'm sorry, St Bartholomew,
that it's turned out this way,
But when the killing ceases,
then we all shall have our day.

Not many of us know about the life of St Bartholomew, or the story of his martyrdom, but we are more likely to be familiar with the St Bartholomew's Day Massacre, which began in Paris in 1572. It occurred to me what a sad thing it is that his designated day each year (24th August) should be forever associated with such an unspeakably brutal episode in human history. *I'm sorry St Bartholomew* was not written as a prayer to a saint, but only addresses him as a means to explore this injustice done unwittingly to a great man of faith, and one of the original twelve chosen by Jesus.

I don't expect, in the great scheme of things, that St Bartholomew is really all that concerned about his own designated day in the year. Among the priorities of heaven, it is a trivial matter, to be sure, sad though it is that human history should be so replete with violence and threat. Along with anyone else who has lived and died faithful to Jesus, his desire would be for the kingdom of God to be established in the world, and for the total destruction of those dark, dehumanising powers that glory in death, vengeance, betrayal and suffering.

It is the reign of Christ on earth that the last verse speaks of – a feast day, surely, to end all feast days.

St Bartholomew

I consider that our present sufferings are not worth comparing with the glory that will be revealed in us. For the creation waits in eager expectation for the children of God to be revealed. For the creation was subjected to frustration, not by its own choice, but by the will of the one who subjected it, in hope that the creation itself will be liberated from its bondage to decay and brought into the freedom and glory of the children of God.
We know that the whole creation has been groaning as in the pains of childbirth right up to the present time. Not only so, but we ourselves, who have the firstfruits of the Spirit, groan inwardly as we wait eagerly for our adoption to sonship, the redemption of our bodies. For in this hope we were saved. But hope that is seen is no hope at all. Who hopes for what they already have?
(Romans 8:18-24)

Abstract Themes

UN-PHILOSOPHY

Nothing is as nothing is,
And nothing as it seems.
To know the truth is not to know
The truth of what it means.
And though the self may not be self,
And all illusion be,
What piles of prose adorn that shelf
marked "Un-philosophy"!

It taunts us with a guarantee:
The universe is bluffing;
And you're a part, if you would see,
Of absolutely nothing.
Outside this universal "Truth",
Our minds being un-enlightened
Will leave us, whether aged or youth,
unrested, troubled, frightened.

Yet all that too, if we but knew,
Is nothing but illusion,
For really suffering isn't true,
Nor sorrow, nor confusion.
And neither can your body be,
Your aching bones, your labour,
The sorrows of your family,
The anguish of your neighbour.

It isn't true since nothing's true,
Enlightened ones will say;
Yet you are here, and you are you,
And this is real, today.
And suffering hurts and hardship strikes,
No matter who denies it –
The teacher teaches what he likes,
But pity him that tries it.

Today's post-modern approaches to truth and reality have not come from nowhere but owe much to ideas of non-being that have surfaced in Europe at various points in history. They exist as a thread within Buddhist teaching, were under discussion among the ancient Greeks, and were proffered to European culture by the Early German Romantics during the late eighteenth century.

Non-being philosophy often underlies claims to offer "inner peace", and it is possible, of course, to see its attraction in this regard. While it may appeal to some, I take the "unenlightened" view that it offers nothing but escapism and false security.

Ideas of non-being stand directly opposed to a biblical understanding of the world. The ministry of Jesus was precisely to acknowledge the world's sufferings and wrongs, and to engage with them. He confronted the God-hating spiritual forces that lie behind the evils we encounter (whether in ourselves, or in others), and this has always been the calling of those who follow him.

Post-modernism would speak of "your truth" and "my truth", as though opposing statements can have equal validity, and should be respected equally, regardless of evidence or reason. Such an approach makes a mockery of justice and robs us of intellectual dignity. It was Pontius Pilate's approach as he allowed himself to be persuaded to condemn Jesus to be crucified.

> *Jesus said, "My kingdom is not of this world. If it were, my servants would fight to prevent my arrest by the Jewish leaders. But now my kingdom is from another place."*
> *"You are a king, then!" said Pilate.*
> *Jesus answered, "You say that I am a king. In fact, the reason I was born and came into the world is to testify to the truth. Everyone on the side of truth listens to me."*
> *"What is truth?" retorted Pilate. With this he went out again to the Jews gathered there and said, "I find no basis for a charge against him…"*
> (John 18:36-38)

NORMAL

People say I'm normal, and that's the goal for me,
With normal friends, and normal clothes
and normal family;
A normal life with normal dreams,
and normal casual talk,
Normal how I wear my hair,
and normal how I walk.

Normal time for exercise, and TV on at night;
Normal heart rate, normal weight
for someone of my height;
Normal diet – can't deny it,
need to watch my drinking;
Normal need to drown the sounds
of thoughts I might be thinking.

Normal Facebook profile, where I hide the real me
In electronic friendships based on unreality;
Don't want to seem dejected on my cyber-lying page;
Why would I? I'm connected –
and I'm normal for my age!

Normal views and normal needs
for games and laughs and action;
Normal Euro-Jackpot hopes and satellite distraction;
People say I'm normal, and normal can be kind;
But normal just avoids
the pressing questions in my mind.

Normal leaves me empty, and normal leaves me dead;
I'm starting to regret that I believed what normal said;
Yes, people say I'm normal, but now I'm not so sure,
And I don't think I want to be so normal anymore.

Conformity can deaden us to the real needs of our lives. Our daily choices of media that we consume, video games that we play, or our "feed" on Facebook or Instagram, can make us numb to any possibilities for our own growth, and blind to opportunities to encourage or assist others.

Routines focused on entertainment and relaxation can cost us and our families dearly as the years pass by. Far better, I think, to ask questions of our lifestyles and preferences, and to wonder why such passive indolence is being pressed upon us. Who gains from our careless spending, or the wasting of our days?

Christian faith demands that we ask hard questions of ourselves and begin to see things in a new light. Understanding and trusting the Father's love for us is a good place to start. It enables us to take hold of his purposes for our lives, and to take back control of our years and our talents. Serving him means nothing less than for us to live out the creative, fruit-bearing calling we've each been given.

"*A man is a slave to whatever has mastered him.*"
(2 Peter 2:19)

THE UNKNOWN KNOWN
AND RUMSFELD'S KNOWLEDGE GRID

" ... *there are known knowns; there are things we know we know. We also know there are known unknowns; that is to say we know there are some things we do not know. But there are also unknown unknowns—the ones we don't know we don't know." (Donald Rumsfeld)*

Knowing that we know a truth
May keep us sane and grounded,
But all our documented proof
Can still turn out unfounded.
We have to keep an open mind,
As things we know we know
Can sometimes make us wholly blind
To what is really so.

It's better for us to perceive
our knowledge unattained;
We fool ourselves if we believe
We're fine with what we've gained.
And what we know we do not know
Brings curiosity,
Out of which new learnings flow,
To prick pomposity.

Things we didn't know we knew
Can bring a certain pleasure,
As scanning deeper depths of view
Surprises us with treasure.
Unknown knowns may lie below
Like some forgotten song;
A prompt, and suddenly we know –
We've known it all along.

But there is knowledge never known
We wouldn't know we lack;
That sees us growing over-blown
And laughs behind our back.
The largest of the sectors here
And darkest of the four,
It forms the root of human fear,
Controversy and war.

With unknown unknowns everywhere
Can ignorance be bliss –
While we're so blindly unaware
That anything's amiss?
Complete and absolute unknowing
Holds us in its thrall,
Obscures our sight of where we're going,
And sets us up to fall.

Placing God within the squares
Will always be contentious,
And metaphysical affairs,
To many, seem pretentious.
To some he's known and others not,
("Known unknown" on the grid),
And "unknown known" where he's forgot
Among the backward-slid.

I wonder if the things of God
Surpass our "knowledge" spheres,
So talk of faith in him seems odd
To unbelieving ears.
He calls us, in the things we know
To maybe look beyond –
A place where many dread to go
And fear they might be conned.

But of a God "unknown unknown"
The Bible doesn't speak,
As in all nature, wisdom's shown
That renders knowledge weak.
The "Unknown God" of ancient Greece
Was Israel's God revealed,
But knowledge doesn't offer peace,
Or see the dead man healed.

<hr />

The knowledge grid existed long before Donald Rumsfeld famously invoked it in the lead-up to the second Iraq War. In his mouth it took on a new, comical quality, as he, the US Secretary of State for Defence, used it as an elaborate way of saying to the world, "We actually know very little". There was nothing funny about the war itself, however, which was a *fait accompli* in any case, regardless of what was known or unknown about Iraq at the time.

This is a poem about the grid's limitations, or at least, the limitations of our own knowledge. Even in areas where we thought we could be certain, we can sometimes later find ourselves to have been misled. Often it's the deceit and bad faith of others that muddies the waters as we make our judgements. Perhaps this is why many avoid Christian religion, fearing that it might only be a means for others to exploit them or to control their lives.

It is true that exploitation and control have played their part in the history of the church and continue to do so. I suggest in the poem that matters of faith may lie outside the knowledge grid, but we do believe in a God who has revealed himself, and who is therefore knowable. The God of the Bible shows himself to be completely faithful. Exploitation, control and deceit are not a part of his character, nor should they be found in anyone who claims to belong to him. Rather, those things belong to the world – to powers that the gospel of Christ would invite us to turn our backs on, and in doing so, to become free.

Paul then stood up in the meeting of the Areopagus and said: "People of Athens! I see that in every way you are very religious. For as I walked around and looked carefully at your objects of worship, I even found an altar with this inscription: TO AN UNKNOWN GOD. So you are ignorant of the very thing you worship—and this is what I am going to proclaim to you..."
(Acts 17: 22-23)

THE MANDELBROT SET

$$z_{n+1} = z_n^2 + C$$

Within the range of 0 to 2 would be
An infinity of points, and each termed "C",
(Minus numbers on both axes too,
For which the same is infinitely true).
And for this function, take a "C" you've read,
And simply add it to the square of "Z".
Since "Z" begins at zero, you'll agree,
Your chosen "C" plus "Z squared" *equals* "C".

The second iteration can now come,
As "Z" will take the value of this sum,
And thus we square it, adding "C" again,
(Beyond this point you're going to need a pen);
And so derive the next "Z" by this mode,
On, to successive iterations in the code.
And sometimes "Z" will rise beyond the set,
Or else it will grow less, and lesser yet.

Reflecting on the axis where they're plotted,
Mandelbrot is famed for what he spotted;
For with his new-attained computer power
And many thousand sums within an hour,
When all the points within his set were seen
Depicted in the graph upon his screen,
Elegant, symmetric, around a beetle's shape,
Emerged a vast and unknown hyperscape.

It took him to a strange and spiralled world
Where elephant and seahorse creatures swirled,
With waves and never-ending tubes of thought,
Designs beyond the power of man to wrought
By art or craft, computer, paint or pen:
Fresh fractals forming now, and now again,
And on and on and even to infinity,
Suggesting, maybe, something of divinity.

And all from one equation, as we've shown,
Whose implications, previously unknown,
Astound us now with beauty and appeal,
Eliciting that sense of awe we feel.
"But number's just a concept", you reply,
"Calculation just a tool that we apply";
We make believe that we're the patent holder;
The universe would tell us, maths is older.

⚬♪⚬ @ ⚬♪⚬

The Bible speaks of God revealing himself through nature, in the beauty of animals and plants, in the intricacy of the workings of our bodies, in the behaviours and instincts of birds and insects. Whether we magnify cells with electron microscopes, or look out to distant stars and planets with our radio telescopes, we cannot help but be struck by the beauty and wonder of creation, and by the wisdom and artistry of the mind of God.

The Mandelbrot Set is entirely theoretical, of course. In itself it is simply an exploration of a mathematical formula. All of life exists as explorations and expressions of mathematical formulae, however, and fractals like those found in the Mandelbrot Set are found in nature, in the structure of snow flakes, in the fronds of ferns, in the forming of islands and in the shaping of clouds.

It is interesting to note that whatever its internal beauty, the patterns of the Mandelbrot set, the elephants, the spirals and the seahorses, are only visible at its margins, where numbers cannot securely stay low, and the set interacts with its non-set surroundings. I cannot help seeing an analogy here with Christian faith, as its life, beauty, vibrance and humanity show themselves best through its messy interactions with the outside, with those not in agreement, with the hurt and the broken in society, and with the unloved.

The heavens declare the glory of God;
* the skies proclaim the work of his hands.*
Day after day they pour forth speech;
* night after night they reveal knowledge.*
They have no speech, they use no words;
* no sound is heard from them.*
Yet their voice goes out into all the earth,
* their words to the ends of the world.*
(Psalm 19: 1-4)

COUNTING

They count,
Weeks and ages;
In Torah's opening pages –
There they count
For tabernacle truth and temple mount;
God's dwelling here: fixed, through faith and fall,
His purposes and Presence in it all.

Seven days,
Closing in rest:
Holy, beautiful and blessed;
And all complete –
Fulfilled, as earth and heaven meet
In Sabbath love! To all the world, a sign
Of faithfulness and hope; of his design.

Forty-nine:
Cycled to the square,
Sabbatical's sabbatical! He's there,
Drawing near
As ram's horns sound the fiftieth year
For sacred liberty and blessed release;
And for the least among his people, peace.

And *they* count,
For there would be
A day for them of *super* Jubilee!
Multiply
Seventy times seven years go by
From Babylon to Galilean shore,
And Israel's God among his own once more.

It is always good to explore the theme of biblical numbers: sabbath (7), sabbatical (7), jubilee (49 and 50), and the recurring 490-year cycle in Israel's history, and how they relate to the presence of God, whether in the Garden of Eden, in the tabernacle and temple, or in the person of Jesus. All of it is bound up in his grace and forgiveness, and so when Jesus is asked how many times a man must forgive his neighbour, his answer is "Not seven times, but seventy times seven." (Matt.18:21-22).

Giving the poem four stanzas, each of them having seven lines, I have tried, in a small way, to echo the Hebrew scribes who so conscientiously made numbers count as they originally set down their scriptures.

The celebration of the year of jubilee required God's people to set free any Israelite that they had taken into servitude, to forgive debt, and to return land to its original owners. It was a mechanism to prevent the gap becoming overly wide between the poor and the rich within their society; a safeguard against the human inclination to accumulate wealth and to disregard the poor. All of it was to ensure that God himself remained at the centre of their lives, and not their wealth, and that he was acknowledged by all his people for his provision and his justice.

Israel's history in the Bible cycles between godly and ungodly leadership, and their readiness to observe the requirements of sabbatical and jubilee serves as a litmus test in the gauging of the sincerity of their religion, however carefully the temple sacrifices and rituals may have been observed. Truly putting God first in our lives requires that we hold our accumulated possessions and our power over others with a very loose grip.

"I hate, I despise your religious festivals;
your assemblies are a stench to me.
Even though you bring me burnt offerings and grain
offerings,
I will not accept them.
Though you bring choice fellowship offerings,
I will have no regard for them.

Away with the noise of your songs!
*   I will not listen to the music of your harps.*
But let justice roll on like a river,
*   righteousness like a never-failing stream!*
(Amos 5:21-24)

He went to Nazareth, where he had been brought up, and
on the Sabbath day he went into the synagogue, as was his
custom. He stood up to read, and the scroll of the prophet
Isaiah was handed to him. Unrolling it, he found the place
where it is written:
"The Spirit of the Lord is on me,
*   because he has anointed me*
*   to proclaim good news to the poor.*
He has sent me to proclaim freedom for the prisoners
*   and recovery of sight for the blind,*
to set the oppressed free,
*   to proclaim the year of the Lord's favour."*
Then he rolled up the scroll, gave it back to the attendant
and sat down. The eyes of everyone in the synagogue were
fastened on him. He began by saying to them, "Today this
scripture is fulfilled in your hearing."
(Luke 4:16-21)

"VAV". THE SIXTH LETTER: "A NAIL"

So the Hebrew scribes
Set out their work as a tabernacle,
That in their written words may dwell
The very presence of God himself.
Every parchment is now a courtyard curtain,
Every column of text, a post,
And at the head of every column,
The nail: *vav,*
The silver hook, holding all together and in place:
Past and future, earth and heaven,
Just as in the beginning, and as it shall be.

And each given workday
Touches the Sabbath at the circle's centre:
Six points of conjunction
In the fullness of all creation.
So *Vav Aleph Vav* amounts to *Mem,*
The *echad* – the oneness of God; living water,
Pregnant with mystery and revelation.
And *mem*'s first stroke is *vav*:
The nail; the shaft of truth.
"Sixteen" signifies love: *yod vav;*
Love as hands and hearts are joined;
Yod, "a hand". Love: a nailed hand.

Isn't it a grammar rule that we should avoid starting sentences with conjunctions? Well it wasn't one the Hebrew scribes had ever heard of – and they had a lot of rules! So I've tried to follow their lead in this reflection on the letter "Vav". It continues the theme of God's temple and tabernacle presence, as the scribes extended it to their own writings: they understood that God was present in and through the inspired Word. (For the main themes of this poem, I am grateful to Aaron Raskin, a YouTube host, although he makes no connection between Vav and the Christian gospel.)

Vav is the letter of connection, the nail that points the way through all of Scripture to the cross of Jesus. He reveals the God of love, the cross is revealed as his sacrifice of love, and the scriptures themselves are revealed to be his communication of love for all humanity.

In the beginning was the Word, and the Word was with God, and the Word was God. He was with God in the beginning. Through him all things were made; without him nothing was made that has been made. In him was life, and that life was the light of all mankind.

[...]

The Word became flesh and made his dwelling among us. We have seen his glory, the glory of the one and only Son, who came from the Father, full of grace and truth.

(John 1:1-4; 14)

FIFTY FEET OF BLESSING

Trace the winding path that brought you here,
Through loveless times, or days of pain and dread;
Sense that troubled journey's end is near –
With fifty feet of floor you've yet to tread.
From open door and through the entrance hall,
Down seated rows of prayer and welcoming face,
And to the cross that's fixed upon the wall:
A world of life in fifty feet of space.

Sacred in the laying down of fears,
Forgiveness, surrendered pride,
And sorrows healed that kept you hunched for years,
And fifty feet of friendship, miles wide;
For here, the living God among his own –
Jesus reflected, body, heart and face;
His glory, truth, and all the love he's shown,
In fifty feet of fellowship and grace.

Not all churches are fifty feet long, but many are around that length. *Fifty Feet of Blessing* was written during a lockdown period, when churches were unable to meet, and I was missing the fellowship. Online services were better than nothing, but they don't compare to the face-to-face contact of real church.

Perhaps my description of church isn't one that you recognise. Churches can sometimes be places where relationships are complex, with brokenness all too evident, and prayer and biblical teaching neglected. They are collections of people, after all!

Even so, enormous possibility for God's healing and restoration exists where the cross is central to Christian fellowship, and where real faith in Jesus translates into genuine love and grace among believers. Such churches do exist, and it is this kind of faithful community that I imagine our visitor discovering for the first time in the opening lines of the poem.

Let us hold unswervingly to the hope we profess, for he who promised is faithful. And let us consider how we may spur one another on toward love and good deeds, not giving up meeting together, as some are in the habit of doing, but encouraging one another—and all the more as you see the Day approaching.
(Hebrews 10:23-25)

TIKTOK WORLD

Hollow hopes,
Tok!
Wasted hours,
TikTok,
Still he waits,
Knock, knock, knock.

Hard weeks pass,
Slap!
Empty praise,
Clap, clap;
Through dull malaise,
Tap, tap, tap.

Changing gears
Click!
Outrunning fears,
Quick! Quick!
All through the years,
Tick, tick, tick.

Yet still he calls,
Hey!
Here I am,
Today! Today!
Walk with me,
My way, My way, My way.

It seems a cruel irony that a phone app designed deliberately to waste the user's time on frivolous and addictive videos should be given the name TikTok. The clock may be ticking, but the user doesn't notice. Constant entertainment by any means robs us of our own personal growth and creativity, and the more we expose ourselves to it, the duller we become.

TikTok World was a response to a study of Ecclesiastes Ch. 2, where the "Teacher" finds dissatisfaction and unfulfillment even in the finest pleasures of life. Jesus is imagined, in my poem, standing at the door as he describes himself in Revelation 3:20, knocking, while lukewarm lives are lived without much reference to him at all. They may "change gear" at certain points with marriage, children, new jobs, or retirement, but those lives are finite. Yet all the time Jesus continues tapping; sometimes he's loud and insistent, most of the time gentle, patient, but always knocking at the doors of our lives. Psalm 95 gives the exhortation, "Today if you hear his voice, do not harden your hearts ...". Now we have time and opportunity to respond to him, but only for a while.

Here I am! I stand at the door and knock. If anyone hears my voice and opens the door, I will come in and eat with that person, and they with me.
(Revelation 3:20)

DISCERNING THE TIMES

Misdirection mocks us,
Unlovingly rocks us –
And babe-like we gurgle our gratitude;
Soothed, softened, smothered,
Maliciously mothered,
In calming and comforting platitude.

Who writes the signs we read?
Where do their roads lead?
And if we dared ask, would they say?
We feed from their spoon
As we dance to their tune,
Singing how we serve God in our day.

A deckchair that someone else puts out,
Must we slump into it – and never doubt
That it will bear us?
Oh, something's
snapped!
The frame and
canvas fold, and we
are trapped.

I am sure that Jesus prayed regularly for the Roman government of his own day. He would have prayed for Herod, the puppet ruler, and Philip his brother, who ruled the territory to the north. He would have prayed for peace and justice in his nation, and for the religious leadership to serve in their positions of power with integrity and genuine faith, representing the interests of the downtrodden instead of enriching themselves.

I don't think he ever assumes good faith among his rulers. Herod was a "fox", and Caesar was to be given only what he was due. The Sanhedrin and the lawyers sought to entrap him and dispose of him. Almost all were opposed to him, spiritually and politically, and Jesus was rightly wary of them.

How should believing communities relate to those who rule over us today? We are commanded to pray for our leaders, just as we would pray for our persecutors. We might hope for good faith among our government advisors and ministers, and among the industrialists who lobby them, but we would be fools to assume it.

Of all people, Bible-believing Christians should be the most alert to misgovernment, and the most willing to question it. I believe it's time we woke up from our TV-addicted stupor. We have recently seen a government "Counter-Disinformation Unit" formed in the UK to police and silence those who cared about open debate and transparency. How long will it be before a similar body is established to censor the Christian message, to silence Christian voices altogether in the public square? Perhaps that work is already well underway, but, like frogs gradually boiled in water, we don't notice as the temperature rises around us.

Praise the LORD.
Praise the LORD, my soul.
I will praise the LORD all my life;
    I will sing praise to my God as long as I live.
Do not put your trust in princes,
    in human beings, who cannot save.
When their spirit departs, they return to the ground;
    on that very day their plans come to nothing.
Blessed are those whose help is the God of Jacob,
    whose hope is in the LORD their God.
He is the Maker of heaven and earth,
    the sea, and everything in them—
    he remains faithful forever.
He upholds the cause of the oppressed
    and gives food to the hungry.
The LORD sets prisoners free,
    the LORD gives sight to the blind,
the LORD lifts up those who are bowed down,
    the LORD loves the righteous.
The LORD watches over the foreigner
    and sustains the fatherless and the widow,
    but he frustrates the ways of the wicked.
The LORD reigns forever,
    your God, O Zion, for all generations.
Praise the LORD.
(Psalm 146)

VOLUMES AND VOLUMES

*(On how many books the whole world would have
room for if all the things Jesus did were written down)*

Twenty eight volumes, six inch by nine,
And three-quarter inch spine-width (with covers),
Will fit in a meter cubed perfectly fine
With one thousand, four hundred others.

For a cubic kilometre, times by a billion,
(1.4 trillion books),
But the space beneath atmosphere's shielding pavilion
Is harder to judge than it looks.

Placing a ceiling 10k from the base,
Earth's atmosphere's size is, they guess,
4.2 billion cubed km of space,
For the books from our infinite press.

So 1.4 trillion, times 4.2 billion
For the number of books it could hold:
Give or take one or two, it's around six sextillion,
That's six thousand trillion, all told.

How many books *would* the whole world have room for, if all the possible testimony of Jesus were written down? Well, in John's day it would have been written on scrolls, anyway, and not in modern-style books. Besides, although it has been interesting to work out how many books would stack into the world's space, it's not really asking the right question of this verse.

A better question would be, What else do we know about, from the Bible, that might actually fill the whole world? Of course, it's the knowledge of the glory of God. This is a recurring theme in the Old Testament, and a promise that it will one day be accomplished. John is deliberately alluding to this, I think, and stating that his own testimony about Jesus, along with everyone else's (so long as it's true), brings fulfilment to this ancient hope.

Concluding his own testimony here in chapter 21, John recalls his introductory theme: "The Word became flesh and dwelt among us." The "Word" is revealed in the life and resurrection of Jesus that John witnessed, and the "knowledge of the glory of God" is spread through the testimony of his people about him, whether through books, scrolls, letters or spoken communication. That testimony continues today, all around the world, in almost every language; life-affirming and life-restoring. The more people try to suppress it, the more powerful and pervasive that testimony becomes, and there will be a time when the glory of God, revealed in Jesus, will finally be known and acknowledged by the whole of his creation.

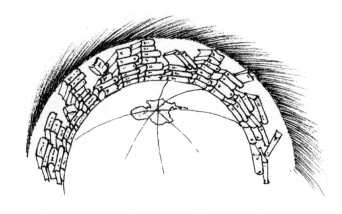

This is the disciple who testifies to these things and who wrote them down. We know that his testimony is true. Jesus did many other things as well. If every one of them were written down, I suppose that even the whole world would not have room for the books that would be written.
(John 21: 24-25)

They will neither harm nor destroy
*   on all my holy mountain,*
for the earth will be filled with the knowledge of the LORD
*   as the waters cover the sea.*
In that day the Root of Jesse will stand as a banner for the peoples; the nations will rally to him, and his resting place will be glorious.
(Isaiah 11:9-10)

Miscellaneous Poems

HANUKKAH

The ancient line of Aaron now stood broken,
Laws of heaven wantonly ignored,
And priestly office nothing but a token:
Authority cared little for the Lord.
Neglect of temple rites; neglect to burn
The sacred offerings – for luxury's appeal!
Loving power but blindly apt to spurn
The power of love; the heart of God to heal.

Syrian alliance reaped its due,
As priestly rulers, lost in all but name
(Reflecting more the Grecian than the Jew),
Lost everything the day the soldiers came.
And who among them thought their compromise
Would lead to desolation and disgrace,
And cause the people zealously to rise
To claim the land and cleanse the Holy Place?

Some would have deemed it all for little gain –
Oppressive rule had rendered them bereft,
But war meant only death and further pain,
And would God even dwell with those it left?
Now miracles are told that all may know
Of armies routed by a rebel band,
And at the temple when the oil was low,
How God supplied the lamp from his own hand.

While victory to the Judeans seemed sweet,
Heed the bitter seed that triumph bore:
Defiance of a force they couldn't beat
Would one day see their scattering once more.
And in the cruse of oil we might suspect,
Though cherished and beloved in its narration,
A seal of God contrived in retrospect;
Nostalgia for an independent nation.

One was worthy, once, to walk that place:
A Shepherd of unbroken royal line
Observed the Feast with gentleness and grace,
But caused offense by claiming the divine.
Yet in this man lay Hanukkah's reward:
Israel's true calling, all that the prophets saw;
Unmuddied waters and untrampled sward;
Anointed rule; fulfilment of the Law.

The Jewish feast of Hanukkah celebrates the re-dedication of the Jerusalem temple in 164 BC. John 10:22-24 tells of Jesus attending the feast in his own day. The Maccabean uprising and the years of self-rule that followed were fondly remembered by the people of Jesus's generation (themselves subject now to Roman rule) but it was a far greater liberty that Jesus embodied, for both Israel and the world.

The gospels speak of him as the ultimate temple, the place where God's presence is located, and where God meets his people. He also represents an uncorrupted priesthood. While the priests are asked, "Must my flock feed on what you have trampled and drink what you have muddied with your feet?" (Ezekiel 34:19), God promises to set a better ruler over Israel. "I will place over them one shepherd, my servant David, and he will tend them ..." (Ezek. 34:23).

There is no record of the "miracle of the cruse of oil" before around AD 500, which suggests that this element of the re-dedication, central to the modern celebration of Hanukkah, is likely to have been concocted by a scribe during the early medieval period.

Then came the Festival of Dedication at Jerusalem. It was winter, and Jesus was in the temple courts walking in Solomon's Colonnade. The Jews who were there gathered around him, saying, "How long will you keep us in suspense? If you are the Messiah, tell us plainly."
Jesus answered, "I did tell you, but you do not believe. The works I do in my Father's name testify about me, but you do not believe because you are not my sheep. My sheep listen to my voice; I know them, and they follow me. I give them eternal life, and they shall never perish; no one will snatch them out of my hand. My Father, who has given them to me, is greater than all; no one can snatch them out of my Father's hand. I and the Father are one."
Again his Jewish opponents picked up stones to stone him, but Jesus said to them, "I have shown you many good works from the Father. For which of these do you stone me?"
"We are not stoning you for any good work," they replied, "but for blasphemy, because you, a mere man, claim to be God."
(John 10:22-33)

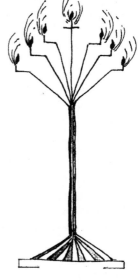

MARCUS AURELIUS HAD A BEARD

Marcus Aurelius had a beard,
And many have copied him since;
A formidable mind and a man to be feared
By Germanic or Parthian prince.

Marcus would write of his taste for the Stoics:
The modest, the manly, the calm;
No interest at all in hot-headed heroics,
Nor flattering, dishonest charm.

Marcus Aurelius sat on his horse,
As statues and stone relief tell;
Equestrian, raised up to rule in due course,
And none of them ruled quite as well.

Un-stirruped Aurelius, rise to the trot!
Oh, you can't? Such a pain in the bum!
Strength through enduring, accepting your lot –
You must bear all, and so overcome.

Bearded Aurelius, Stoic and sure,
Constant and noble and brave!
He bothered in government, bothered in war,
But he couldn't be bothered to shave.

Marcus Aurelius, reigning from AD 161 to 180, is known as the philospher-emperor. He was much revered during the "Enlightenment" of the 18th century and is still held in high esteem as a non-Christian exemplar of fine leadership. Aurelius is famous for his adoption of Stoicism and Greek mystery religion. He's also famous for his beard.

Regardless of how he might have compared with other Roman emperors (he was among the better of them), or how noble his principles were (some of them were very noble), his, I would say, was not a life well-lived.

Stoicism can be found in the teachings of dead churches throughout the world, where ancient Greek notions of "duty" and endurance are substituted for the freeing gospel of love

and relationship with the Father. It is only within the context of that love and freedom in Christ, that we can usefully consider any of those ideals so cherished by Marcus Aurelius, and in a Christ-centred approach they take on a completely different character, with different priorities and a wholly different spirit.

His pleasure is not in the strength of the horse,
*   nor his delight in the legs of the warrior;*
the LORD delights in those who fear him,
*   who put their hope in his unfailing love.*
(Psalm 147:10-11)

So whether you eat or
drink or whatever you do,
do it all for the glory of
God.
(1 Corinthians, 10:31)

50 MILES AN HOUR

In my six-year-old mind, 50 miles an hour
Was the final achievement of motorised power;
Eyes wide with the thrill of the engine's roar
As we travelled to school in our brown Renault 4.

If a friend with a new car came to school with his dad,
I wasn't concerned with what model he had,
Or whether his buy was expensive or thrifty.
No. All that I cared was, Could it do fifty?

My dad would do fifty, (my mum wouldn't quite,
As the farm lanes were narrow and corners
were tight),
And sometimes he'd sing as he went through the gears
Some song, half-remembered from army years.

And the back of our Renault 4 never seemed tight
With us three sat together, and we'd argue and fight;
Legs always in range of a sudden smack,
If we were too rowdy while sat in the back.

No seat belts, of course, but no one was scared,
As back in the seventies nobody cared,
But now that I'm older, these two things I know:
That seat belts make sense, and that 50's quite slow.

The idea of "going round corners at fifty miles an hour" fascinated me as a child, and I would ask my mother what she thought about it. I was always disappointed by her answer, of course, which I thought at the time to be overly cautious. When, during imaginary chases, my toy Batmobile took corners (marked out by the pattern on our floor rug), it was always at 50 miles an hour. A ride in our family's brown Renault 4 wasn't quite the same, but exciting, nonetheless.

Fifty miles an hour may be slow by today's standards (at least, on faster roads), but we take for granted speeds of travel that were unthinkable in human history before my grandparents' generation. The danger of cutting travel time, perhaps, is that we learn to despise the journey, and to value only the destination. These verses were written only as a reminiscence of my childhood, but by way of Christian reflection here, it is good, at times, to question our attitudes to inconveniences and impediments that we encounter in life. The God of the Bible is always interested in the direction and purpose of our lives, whether we find ourselves in a season of frantic busyness, or one of relative quiet. His involvement enables us to appreciate the pace of our journey – the fast and exhilarating times as much as the hard-going stretches, where we're forced to slow down. He's interested in the growth of our character in all situations, and our resolve, above all, to remain focused on him.

*Therefore, since we are surrounded by such a great cloud
of witnesses, let us throw off everything that hinders and
the sin that so easily entangles. And let us run with
perseverance the race marked out for us, fixing our eyes on
Jesus, the pioneer and perfecter of faith. For the joy set
before him he endured the cross, scorning its shame, and
sat down at the right hand of the throne of God.*
(Hebrews 12:1-2)

PERSIAN LAMENT

Imposed upon the peaceful hour of dawn,
The unrelenting, unbidden call to prayer
Reaffirms subjection, as to warn
That here pervade the rulers of the air.
And here men follow as they know they must,
Convinced that in their following, they're free;
For Arab laws and customs, ever just,
Reward compliant religiosity.

Yet many here resent the cheap charade,
As rulers rule with kleptocratic shame –
And place their hope in execution yard
And torture cell to keep the people tame.
But into man-made chaos Jesus speaks,
And many find forgiveness by his hand,
For now a false and godless regime creaks
Beneath impending judgement on its land.

Judged will be the judges and the courts,
The cruel apparatus of control,
Policing minds and hearts, patrolling thoughts,
But impotent against the honest soul.
And on afflicted saints God's Spirit rests –
Heaven's hope in hiding place or jail,
Encouragement to hold fast through the tests
Where human strength and worldly will would fail.

It is hard to know the true number of Christian believers in Iran, as so much of the church operates in secret, with the possibility of raids on their meetings, arrests, torture, and even the threat of execution for those who have converted from Islam. Many believers are currently being held in Iranian prisons, and some have died. They are not alone as victims of the regime; threat, violence and injustice is meted out to any who dare question its policies, especially regarding opportunities for women. My poem is about Christian belief in Iran, but it's a lament for the whole nation, for all who have suffered under misrule there, recognising enormous courage and spirit among a people who refuse to be broken.

Despite persecution and misgovernment, however, great numbers of Iranian men and women have turned to Christ in recent years. Where bibles are scarce and Christian teachings suppressed, many Iranians encounter Jesus in dreams or in visions, only subsequently to read of him in the gospels, or to hear of him at Christian gatherings. By whatever means they discover him, it is a cause for thanks and celebration. In the prisons, too, many believers testify to the powerful ways God has sustained them, and enabled them to continue to hold to his truth, all the more convinced of it, even under the worst of conditions.

Keep on loving one another as brothers and sisters. Do not forget to show hospitality to strangers, for by so doing some people have shown hospitality to angels without knowing it. Continue to remember those in prison as if you were together with them in prison, and those who are mistreated as if you yourselves were suffering.
(Hebrews 13:1-3)

NOW YOU'RE HERE

I might seem resistant, brooding, distant,
(Though I probably haven't come far),
But everything's new, and I've never met you,
And I don't have a clue who you are.

You couldn't know the horrors I've seen,
What I've lived, how I've hurt, and hurt still;
And could anyone like the person I've been?
Will you hate me? You probably will.

******

You're safe in this nest; live at ease, unstressed,
Without worry or shouting or fear;
Love sees the best while forgiving the rest,
Live in calm, free from harm, now you're here.

The theme of adoption runs unmistakably through the New Testament. It is bound up with the experience of turning to Christ in faith, as we acknowledge God as our "Father", and we take on a new identity as believers which we would have had no right or access to if Jesus hadn't secured it.

Now You're Here imagines the thoughts of a cared-for child arriving at the door of his or her new family, to be housed with them and to be raised by them. Perhaps some of the child's feelings touched on in the poem might echo those of a new believer joining a church for the first time, wondering how they might be received and whether they'll even be liked.

The third verse seeks to answer those worries and doubts in the voice of the child's new carers. Life is complicated, and children can be challenging, but broadly this would be an ideal for the care that any fostering or adopting family would hope to provide. In much the same way, a new believer should have his or her fears quickly laid to rest, as the church's role is to support them in their growth, and to offer them love, not judgement.

> For those who are led by the Spirit of God are the children of God. The Spirit you received does not make you slaves, so that you live in fear again; rather, the Spirit you received brought about your adoption to sonship. And by him we cry, "Abba, Father." The Spirit himself testifies with our spirit that we are God's children. Now if we are children, then we are heirs—heirs of God and co-heirs with Christ, if indeed we share in his sufferings in order that we may also share in his glory.
> (Romans 8:14-17)

Printed in Great Britain
by Amazon

35552231R00076